TRIUMPH HOUSE
Poetry with a Purpose

JOURNEYS TO THE SOUL

Edited by

CHRIS WALTON

First published in Great Britain in 1998 by
TRIUMPH HOUSE
1-2 Wainman Road, Woodston,
Peterborough, PE2 7BU
Telephone (01733) 230749

All Rights Reserved

Copyright Contributors 1998

HB ISBN 1 86161 388 1
SB ISBN 1 86161 383 0

FOREWORD

Many people are taking a wider interest in the special gift of writing poetry. *Journeys To The Soul* is a perfect example of how the authors use this medium to express their deepest feelings and emotions to others.

Opening the pages of this book is like opening a doorway into the creative minds of our Christian authors, enabling them to share their thoughts on life and the world around them. Together the poets unite to show their compassion and faith, forming a single voice that reflects the views of Christians all over the world.

Editor
Chris Walton

CONTENTS

The Flame Of Earth	David Fairweather	1
Respite	Georgina Francis McKellar	2
A Tapestry Of Life	Maureen Josie Archibold	3
Rescued	A V R Cracknell	4
Oh Heavenly Child Of Bethlehem	Geraldine Squires	5
To Bed With The Lord	Sharon Howells	6
Listen With God	Peggy Howe	7
Childhood Remembered	J P Paterson	8
The Key To Our Hearts	Wendy Watkin	9
Brokenness	Georgina Dixon	10
Tough Connection	J Baker	11
The Symbol	Lyn Mitchell	12
The Smile	Robert Moore	13
My Ceaseless Thirst	Marion Staddon	14
The Sower	L Thompson	15
Journey To The Soul	David M Grant	16
Handing The Reins Over	Pat Melbourn	17
Our Song	G Ritchie	18
Childhood Memories	Dawn Parsons	19
My Samaritan	Claire Young	20
Always There	Cath Johnston	21
The Body Of Christ	Caroline Mortimer	22
For You This Is My Prayer	Don Mayle	24
I Wish I Had . . .	Adrian Evans	25
Memory	Alison Carr	26
Love Everlasting	Mary Anne Scott	27
Made Out Of Trees	G Bremner	28
The Agnostic	Laura McEwing	29
Up The Wooden Hill	John Wiltshire	30
Grandma And Grandad's Christmas Party	M E Smith	31
Christ Really Cares . . .	Philip Anthony Corrigan	32
Heaven	Don Goodwin	33
Love Personified	R D Hiscoke	34
Swimming Against The Tide	Heather Kirkpatrick	35

Love So Vast And Free	Norah Page	36
Chirpy Childhood 1919	James Leonard Clough	37
Friend To A Failure	Jim Carson	38
Untitled	James Henry Brown	39
Seeking	A J Butterworth	40
He Gave Me Grace	Rebecca Coombs	41
Dive In Deep	Scott Turner	42
Preferred Images	Perry McDaid	43
Six Months Clean	Twinny	44
Love Eternal Love	N Yogaratnam	45
The Guardian	G J Outhwaite	46
To Keith	Elizabeth Mary McNally	47
Faith Hope Charity	K C Thomas	48
Our World	Sadie Williams	49
A Seed Remains	Angela Butler	50
Old Man	Meg Turnbull	52
In The Mountain Of My Dreams	Paul Gainsford Bailey	53
Lonely	Victoria Wills	54
Real Christmas	Nance Davies	55
Hope	Kathleen Davey	56
Delta Moment: Egypt 1943	Eric Smart	57
Thank you For Being My Friend	Michael D Kearney	58
A Silent Prayer	Doreen Petherick Cox	59
Childhood Relived	Jean Bishop	60
Jesus	Bob Shepherd	62
Street Song	Dorothy Neil	63
A Fine Week	S J Davidson	64
No Ordinary Tree	Elizabeth McWilliam	65
Prayer Share	Ann Voaden	66
The People's Princess - (1961-1997)	A Jones	67
The Dying Thief	Stan Mundy	68
Needlework	D M L Ranson	69
Alcohol - The Hidden Beast	Elaine Carver	70
Amos Barker	A C Stock	71
The Ghosts Of Old Poems	Marion Schoeberlein	72
I To The Hills	Ian Meredith	73

The Cross	J Whitehouse	74
Memories	Maimie Stokoe	76
Heart Revival	Natalie Brocklehurst	77
Our Life On Earth	Margaret Meadows	78
Behold The Lamb Of God	Vera Smith	79
In Your Hands	Kim Montia	80
His Everlasting Arms	Teresa Steele	81
Wings Of An Angel	Gerry Howsin	82
Easter	Heather Graham	83
On The Beach	Paul Sherbird	84
God's Answer	O Savage	85
One Year Of Peace In Northern Ireland	O Wylie	86
Your Presence	Penelope Jayne Hopkins	87
A Thanksgiving For Light	Elizabeth Mary Crabtree	88
A Prayer - With All My Love - Meg	Meg Brighton	89
Watch And Pray	Louie Conn	90
Circle Line	James Ivor Jones	91
A Cry From My Heart	Mark Barnes	92
Field Of Dreams	Carol Carthy	94
Born Abroad	Christine-Louise Secretan	95
The Tree	Alma Taylor	96
Mosi-Oa-Tunya	Zoé Hodges	97
Gentle Mary	John G Kingsley	98
From My Sitting Room Window	Rene Slack	99
A Post Christian-Era Lament	Sarah Knox	100
Faith	Hannah Birch	102
Only A Piece Of Clay	Henry Armstrong	103
God Ain't Dead	Colin E Amey	104
Thoughts Of Freedom	Julie Howick	105
Preaching To Myself	Val Flint-Johnson	106
Silent Wings	Morag Oag	107
Prepare For War	Caroline Mortimer	108
Pattern Of Life	Betty Furneaux	109
A Blessing On The House	Lesley Player	110
Judas	Deryck Mason	111
Eve Of Construction?	Judy Studd	112

THE FLAME OF EARTH

To keep alive the flame of faith
is what a writer said.
This must be done throughout the years
in times both good and bad,
and though we know
that those who gifted with the verse
wrote poetry and sacred hymns
to keep alive the flame of faith,
it is the unknown, unsung
daily saints who unremembered are
who make the continuity
of Christian life in Church and Chapel
burn afresh in each generation
through every new congregation
praising God in word and song
from those who gifted with the verse
wrote poetry and sacred hymns
to keep alive the flame of faith.

David Fairweather

RESPITE

Dear Heaven I need respite care
A Haven of Hope
When I can no longer bear
The strain of being a Christian, where,
So many are fighting for a share
Of earth's dull glory, and I must declare
I need shelter in His tender care.

Earthly friends wearied by the year
Have forsaken the common prayer.
For the sake of my spiritual welfare
Will He now, so just and so fair
Take my hand and lead me there
Resuscitate my faith anew, dare
I Aspire to Respite Care?

Georgina Francis McKellar

A Tapestry Of Life

In the alcoves of my mind -
Memories abide
Some of laughter and of joy,
Some of heartache and of tears.
Through it all I held my head up high
For I'm trusting in my Lord
No matter what, He upholds me
In the tapestry of life
Bright colours hold to the dark threads
For in losing loved ones in life
Or sadly in death.
The canvas will unfold
God's tapestry of life
That one day joy will return
He's set a pattern for my life
For eternal love goes on forever
Jesus swept cobwebs away
He alone had set me free.

Maureen Josie Archibold

RESCUED

No rescue needed, the skies are blue
The sea is calm and smooth
The ship is whole and proud
Gliding fearlessly into the future.

Life is a voyage in many ways
Sometimes smooth and pleasant
Riding on a high or low
While passing through the straits of life

Voyaging in isolation
Far away from kith and kin
Worthwhile lessons to be learnt
But sometimes very hard.

Life, like sailing has its dangers
Storm and tempest, wild and free,
Gaining, losing, sometimes winning,
Everything but life is gone.

Holding on whate'er the prospects
Life once lost, can never be regained
Brave, courageous, folk will rescue
Those that know they're lost.

Still there is the gleam of hope
Someone called the Saviour, knows your plight
This is, oh so great salvation,
To be saved when all seemed lost.

A V R Cracknell

OH HEAVENLY CHILD OF BETHLEHEM

Oh heavenly Child of Bethlehem
be with us here today,
send down your grace into this place
and bless us all, we pray;
for at this Christmas season it is to you we turn;
we contemplate your Holy state
and with new hope we burn.

To shepherds keeping lonely watch
upon the hillside there,
angels proclaim your lowly birth
in homely stable bare.
For orient kings a star did shine
to lead them on their way.
We join with them to worship you;
offer our love today.

Geraldine Squires

TO BED WITH THE LORD

Blow out the candle, let's sleep for the night,
The guardian angels are shedding their light,
As the moon gently saunters its way through the air
The Lord will be watching and sending His care.
A tiara of sunlight rockets up through the sky
Then drifts far away till daytime is nigh,
The whole universe looks just like a book,
Or a photograph shining when first it was took,
But no picture *could* shine or portray things like these,
As the tears in my eyes dance in the breeze.

Sharon Howells

LISTEN WITH GOD

If for you the sun is hiding,
If for you a cloud is there,
If you think your heart is breaking,
Not a friend to feel or care.

Lift your eyes up to the Heavens,
Kneel and say a little prayer.
No need to feel so sad and lonely,
Remember God is always there.

He will find the time to listen,
You're always safe within His hands.
His open arms are there to comfort,
No questions asked, and no demands.

Someone out there needs a handshake,
Someone out there needs a smile.
This is what the Lord will tell you,
For giving, makes your life worthwhile.

God gave you life, so use it wisely,
Put your courage to the test.
When at last the great call comes,
You'll know that you have done your best.

Peggy Howe

CHILDHOOD REMEMBERED

When I was little, time was big;
Five minutes wait a dragging misery;
An hour to play with friends a long, long time
And yet, however long, not long enough.

The holidays stretched out, it seemed, forever,
Yet one day lost was cause for childish tears.
There was time to look, to wonder and enquire
But yet the day was never long enough.

Next year was never, but next year did come.
The world and time slowly began to shrink.
Year followed year. What was infinity
Became more comprehensible.

A wider circle, more relationships;
Friends, those more distant and the others
Who frightened me. I learned to value friendship.
Life opened out before me. I was growing up.

J P Paterson

THE KEY TO OUR HEARTS

Always know,
Someone is there,
Never worry,
He will care.
We're provided with helpers,
To unlock our heart
To free us from problems,
And make a new start.

The key to our heart is a precious thing,
Only God knows the joy it can bring.
So don't be afraid to let Him in,
To cleanse your soul from within.
His angels are always there to be found,
Wafting happiness all around.

Wendy Watkin

BROKENNESS

The pain, the pain O Lord, the pain
Tearing and gnawing inside.
Shut off - walls surround me.
My heart is troubled deep within;
I need to be reconciled with you Lord,
But I can't, I can't confess it out!

My child, I love you so you need to let go
Of all those hurts and fears.
Speak out the things that are holding you back
In sharing my joy - come to me.
Take my hand, trust me to guide you through
The doorway to freedom.
There is no condemnation; Jesus paid the price.
He gave His love, forgiveness and sacrifice.

Georgina Dixon

TOUGH CONNECTION

Dear operator please give me a direct line,
I don't seem to be able to get through.
The line is always busy and I don't feel fine,
Please help, I just don't know what else to do.

Please don't give me St Peter's extension number,
Nor that of Angel Gabrielle for he will not do.
I am told our Heavenly Father is never in slumber,
Yet I'm still having trouble getting through.

I do understand operator if you're not willing,
If you're a non-believer I am sure He will listen to you
So please connect my call. Keep the phone ringing.
I'll be in your debt if you'll just put me through.

All I hear is static on the line no words of wisdom.
Who the hell am I kidding? He has not the time
When He has to take care of billions in His kingdom.
Sorry operator I guess I just got a little out of line.

J Baker

THE SYMBOL

Set free the white dove
as a symbol of my love
I give you my heart
It's yours until we part
every beat is yours forever
loving you always
forgetting you never
so take heed my sweetheart
no other can tear us apart
but come what may
I'm yours forever and a day

Lyn Mitchell

THE SMILE
(A tribute to my son, Paul)

It was the radiance of sunshine,
It brought the light on a dark and dismal day.
In its presence you felt serene and comfortable,
You always felt . . . it should never go away
Worries and troubles deserted your mind,
Feeling of sadness left you, you became refined.
A yearning for this emotion will always be there,
The memory of this vision he left behind.
The vibes this vision created was felt by one and all.
What was this magic that brought these lovely feelings?
. . . No more than the smile of my son Paul.

Robert Moore

My Ceaseless Thirst

As a deer pants for a water brook
My soul pants for my Lord above.
Aware of my deep inner-thirst
I walk in ways of His love.

At the core of my being
My Lord resides,
I believe in Him forever
Till all rivers run dry.

Deep in my craving
For His water divine,
I long after you Lord
Till the end of my time.

On my way as I walk with You
I will tell others,
Then in Your Kingdom
I will have sisters and brothers.

The deer shall leap
With the Lamb of High,
Like a swooping hawk
In the blue sky.

Marion Staddon

THE SOWER

Before the farmer plants his crop
The soil must be dug and cleared,
So the seed of The Word must also fall
In ground that's been prepared.
As the spade digs deep to turn and lift,
To loosen and expose,
So the mind expands as we fellowship,
When trust and friendship grows.
As rocks in the soil to the surface rise
So the heart yields to interest shown,
Then a listening ear and a caring heart
Will remove every rock and stone.
As the soil is cleared, all debris gone,
It's time to remove the weeds -
All teaching that's not from our Lord -
Wrong thoughts, beliefs and creeds.
Then feed the soil with the nutrients
Of right teaching, truth and The Word.
When the soil, enriched, has all it needs,
Then it's time to plant the seeds.
Just one more thing, a good watering
As the Holy Spirit flows.
Then God will provide, all that's required,
As the seed in secret grows.

L Thompson

JOURNEY TO THE SOUL

From a place, I never knew,
To a time before I grew.
When going home was strong,
And life was way too long.

The journey through the mist,
That love, I never kissed,
Of feelings almost known,
In a time not yet full grown.

I'm crying in the rain,
And leave behind the pain,
Of storms once tossed and turned,
Those lessons cruelly learned.

My heart, it aches to know,
How far this trek must go,
Will nature's breath be kind,
Or leave me way behind.

In hope and silence now,
I take my final bow,
The journey almost done,
As slips the setting sun,
Beyond the burning hills,
Of broken dreams and wills.

The twilight of my years,
Those shedding, dying tears,
That strengthened, length of time
To sweeten bitter wine.

David M Grant

HANDING THE REINS OVER

Nothing can be done about
The world and all its sin -
Unless the Holy Spirit comes
To dwell in each, within.

And if we are obedient
To the Word of God each day -
A faith that's strong and comforting
Will be given as we pray.

Feelings can mislead us
If the Spirit is not heeded -
And so we are far 'too low'
To act when it is needed.

Emotion must be prayed for -
The anger and the hurt
As feelings pull us down so much
To make us hard and curt.

Faith rests in the power of God -
Not for us to be in control -
For He has planned our lives for us
But *we* keep on setting the goal.

So much sorrow from our own minds -
Recalling events of the past -
And yet if we let God take the reins -
We'll find that our faith will last.

For God will work our purposes out
And such goodwill come out of bad -
But this is His work and ours to 'trust'.
Have joy in this and be glad.

Pat Melbourn

OUR SONG

How can a song, spiral or belong
Notes singing out
Tunes to and from
Make you feel lonely
Memories awash with old thoughts and new
Or feeling brand new
This concept of music, stinging your brain
Singing and dancing
Outwards, in the rain
Wrestling emotions of
Girls you once loved
Heaven above
Knows of your songs
Closing my eyes, back there again
Holding her close, dancing embrace
Her breath in my face
Holding her tight, I can't let it go
The still of this night
So nearing twilight
Thoughts are awash, memories aflow
The song still plays on
Regardless of whom.

G Ritchie

CHILDHOOD MEMORIES

From a window in my mother's room
As a child I'd stand and look
Across the fields where I could see
A gentle flowing brook.
I remember a farmer and his dog
Riding on their cart
Wild rabbits playing in the lane
Under a hedge would dart.

In the evening as the sun sank low
Out a shepherd and his dog would go
To bring the sheep all safely home
Not one was ever left alone.
I could hear the shepherd's voice call out
And watch the collie run about.

The shepherd was a great big man
With gentle hands he carried a lamb.
The sheep all safe within their fold
But onto this lamb he tightly holds.

In many parts of the world today
The country life has passed away.
But here in my memories I recall
The farmer and this shepherd tall.

These things I've remembered over the years,
To sometimes shed a silent tear.
For the years that sped away too soon
And the child that stood in her mother's room.

Dawn Parsons

My Samaritan

I was drowning in a sea of despair,
Until I saw you, there
Offering your warm hand to me,
Squeezing mine, so lovely,
Kind words came from your lips,
As you stroked my hair with your fingertips,
Telling me my problems would all go away,
Turning my night-time into a bright new day,
Helping me to find faith,
Within my heart, again,
Comforting me and helping me,
Overcome my pain.

Claire Young

ALWAYS THERE

You're always there to lend a hand
You're always there to understand
You're always there when things get tough
You're always there when I feel rough
You're there when I'm feeling sad
You're always there when I'm glad
Thank You Jesus for always being there
You're wanted
You're loved
You really do care

Cath Johnston

THE BODY OF CHRIST

Unity in diversity,
Members of a family,
Different parts but one perfect whole;
The Body of Christ we do behold.

We all have our different gifts;
Our aim is the Church to uplift.
Although each part is different,
Each one from the Lord is sent.
For each God has a special plan,
To finish the work that He began.

God's Will is not that we should vaunt,
But to remember we're all blood-bought.
No-one is better than all the rest,
God never makes anyone second-best.

A foot was never meant to be a hand,
Both are equally in demand.
Ever tried walking without your feet
And without hands who could you greet?
Without your eyes you'd miss your way,
And without your mouth you nothing could say.

There are parts of the body that no-one can see,
But without them where would we be?
Often these are the most needed,
So don't think you've not succeeded.

Just because you don't think you can preach,
Doesn't mean you shouldn't go on the outreach.
God can anoint
What to you disappoints.
God makes opportunities out of our failings,
And gives us victories daily.

So let's stop comparing ourselves with each other.
God didn't make us to be like our brother.
He has a great purpose for you and for me.
So let's pray that we His purpose do see.

Caroline Mortimer

FOR YOU THIS IS MY PRAYER

All things bright and beautiful
This is my prayer for you
Just place your hand, in His strong hand
And let Him take you His way through.

He will set you in Heavenly places
He will show you the stairway to climb
And as together you climb the stairway
He will hold you and say 'You are Mine.'

He has loved you since the day you were born
His love is beyond compare
When you're feeling cast down, He can lift you up.
For you this is my prayer.

He is the rose of Sharon,
He is the fairest of the fair.
May you find His love and peace within.
For you this is my prayer.

He knows your struggles, your pain and your fear
He can touch your heart when you're feeling sad
He is a God that will wipe every tear
And He will make your heart glad.

Let not your heart be troubled
He will lift you from despair
He will hold you close, in His everlasting arms.
For you this is my prayer.

Let His love surround you
Something wonderful He will surely prepare
He will make a way for you.
For you this is my prayer.

Don Mayle

I Wish I Had . . .

Posted the blow that delivered you from your feet.
Planted the boot that cultured a leaf-green bruise
across your ribs and ensured you lay,
long enough to ponder . . .

the untruths told which escaped you
from an ailing matrimony, and cast me
asunder, into some crater,
its depths beyond those of depression,
but too shallow to escape me an audience.

Adrian Evans

MEMORY

As I glance,
At the wire,
I remember the past,
Barbed,
I recall things,
I could not,
Should not,
Be able to remember

Trenches,
Plastered in dampness,
Muddied,
Bullet-ridden,
Laden with soldiers,
Sodden army uniforms,
Of scarlet marked chests

Resisting,
Conscientious objectors,
Of the suffering of war,
As they wilt with battle fatigue

Memories of landing,
Wading through water,
Crashing off landing craft,
To dive into cover,
To ward off German fire,
As bullets and weapons,
Fire slivering the air with light,
Yellowing the air with its warning call,
As it cuts through breathing.

Alison Carr

LOVE EVERLASTING

Sometimes when I feel lonely
I just say a little prayer,
As I am never all alone
There's always someone there.

Someone who loves me truly
No matter what I do,
He is my forever friend
And he loves everyone else too.

His love is everlasting
Though at times He must feel sad,
As we all tend to ignore Him
Except when things are bad.

So . . . I try to remember
To thank Him every day,
To ask Him to care for all my friends
That's why I like to pray.

No special words or formula
I just speak to Him as a friend,
You see . . . I don't want to be a stranger
When I meet Him . . . at the end!

Mary Anne Scott

Made Out Of Trees

I cast my mind back, years ago
To a story told to me
Of Noah and his family
And an Ark made out of trees

The good Lord spoke to Noah
He did tell him it would rain
To build an Ark, and stay afloat
It would save him loss and pain

For forty nights and forty days
The rains came pouring down
Yet his family and their wives were safe
And the animals did not drown

Then one day a dove returned
With a twig held in its beak
Noah fell upon his knees
And the good Lord he did greet

Now to this land he trotted out
The animals he set free
Now to this day we all must thank
That Ark he made from trees.

G Bremner

THE AGNOSTIC

Faith and glory,
  an unknown story,
uncertainty, for me runs deep,
  belief, a non-issue,
  Religion, my youth,
  in truth
      needed proof,
  in times of need,
      a lonely person indeed.

Laura McEwing

UP THE WOODEN HILL

Now listen children
all you brothers and sisters,
whatever colour
you are, and your pets as well.
Many years ago
in the age of 'dot'
I was born, and my
name is John.
Now having reached
seventy I can funnily
enough remember
my childhood, and pets, and friends,
and so will you, God willing.
My Father used to
give me a 'piggy back'
to that song - long forgotten -
and he and my Mother
tucked me into bed
and said 'God bless you son'
but not before
I had said my prayers.
I said them, being very young,
'God bless Dad and Mum -
God bless my friends and pets
all over the world
and finally God bless me as well'
and just as I fell asleep
I said to my cat,
'God Bless Susie.'

John Wiltshire

GRANDMA AND GRANDAD'S CHRISTMAS PARTY (AT THE FARM)

My mam and I would get ready on this special day -
Whatever weather was and would likely to be
We were always there when Grandma made Christmas tea!
All the cousins went in the parlour first and
  she'd open box of chocs -
Oh we enjoyed them all out of this fancy box!
Grandad threw in the crackers and we pulled and they went *bang!*
Then we all went into the kitchen in our fancy hats and sang -
There was the plates with cake and mince pies and chicken
All of us were hungry and then we clambered in
To the sitting room decorated with cards and a tree
We all looked forward to this when we were all so wee.

Aunty Sally was staying there, she lived across the miles -
Then my cousin Don walked through the door -
I had never seen him before and he kissed me under the mistletoe!
We were so young not barely seven, but now I still will write
Across the miles after sixty years, our lifestyles had changed
  over all those years.
When tea was over, Grandad would play his usual game -
I remembered this over my younger days, it was always just the same.
Next Christmas cousin Don was not there, back in SA he was,
But I shall always remember it was the first time I had been kissed
A sweet thought it was one I would have missed.

Most of those people are no longer here - God took them from us
They were all so dear - except Don he comes over nearly every year.
The cousins are still here they took the farm,
But the memories remain of our childhood days
When Grandma and Grandad invited us all to the Christmas party.
They were all so cheerful and hearty.

M E Smith

CHRIST REALLY CARES...

Sister Sue looking so sad,
Same week losing mum and dad.
Sitting staring at those walls,
Tragedy struck at those falls.

Went walking on a summer day,
Hillside caved in, swept them away.
Talking to sis, she seems unaware,
All day in her nightie, not even there.

Since that day no word spoken,
Weeping but still silence unbroken.
Feeling the loss with deep sorrow,
I know they say there's no tomorrow.

In troubles of grief, God's love for thee,
In such tragedy, it well may be.
Of two defeats, two are despair,
Prayers are said, Christ really cares.

Philip Anthony Corrigan

HEAVEN

I have been to Ireland, to Killarny's Lakes and Dells.
I have been to Winchester, and heard them ring the bells.
I have been to Scotland, to the mountains and the moors.
I have been in prison behind those bars and doors.
I have lived in England, with its roses and its lawns.
I have been to Yarmouth, and tasted sea fresh prawns.
I have had a glimpse of Heaven, where none above do match.
Even the roses of old England, are not even a patch
On the gardens of Heaven, where I went that special day.
There I spoke with Jesus, and this He had to say.
'Tell them that I'm real, and I am alive and well,
And if they repent and follow Me, then with Me they will dwell.'

Don Goodwin

LOVE PERSONIFIED

Dare I with love surround you on this the happiest of days
As we shared with many good wishes and most of all praise
In that wondrous splendour as everything is correct and right
We all marvel as you surrender to this your birthday dear so bright
Could I bring further happiness and this glorious day entertain
Far afield and very near those greetings resound the same
Congratulations are in order especially at this stage
For you have reached one hundred years a most pleasant age.

None shall mar the gathering as we all salute you true
Greetings from Her Majesty a telegram designed for you
What a wonderful honour at this grand old age
You are so wise and unpredictable more so than any sage
One hundred years old today do they know the truth?
Bearing in mind one's faculties here is the living proof
Of a memory still remarkable and a hand that could rule the waves
This grand matriarch of history could still detail every page

No illness except the odd ache and pain associated with growing old
No diet but a sensible appetite all these wonders now unfold
Exercise of both body and mind hence these remarkable results
An occasional small wee toddie to stimulate medically of course

R D Hiscoke

SWIMMING AGAINST THE TIDE

When I was at my lowest ebb, swimming against the tide
It was then I called to Him, and He swam by my side
For many years I only called, when I was in dismay
I never really bothered, when things were going my way
Yet when I called to Him, He still had time for me
He kept my head above the water, He could have cast me free
There have been many times, when I have let Him down
In spite of all my failings, He's never let me down
As I sail on through my life, I know I will get wet
He'll send the sun and wind to dry me, then quickly I'll forget
To thank Him just for being there, when I need Him most
Helping me to navigate, until I reach the coast.

Heather Kirkpatrick

LOVE SO VAST AND FREE

It was from death's dark valley
Encompassed by shadows of night
That Jesus led me by the hand
Into His Kingdom of Light.

He brought me to His banqueting house -
His banner o'er me was love
He taught me love that conquers all
A love that comes from above

He gave me His Holy Spirit
Greatest love I have ever known
Since He came into my life
I am His and His alone

How can I ever repay Him
For this love that He's given me?
'Take it to the world, He said
'this love so vast and free.'

Norah Page

CHIRPY CHILDHOOD 1919

Born in the fine rugged Pennine scenery,
With lusty snowstorms weighing down greenery;
After a blizzard our hills were silver-bright,
On home-made toboggans we raced till moonlight.

Indoors we had no toy train with electrics,
We made the most of wooden coloured square bricks;
Building castles, defence forts and huge towers,
Red Indians and cowboys manoeuvred for hours.

Our hide-out was an old rundown stone stable,
Furnished with worn matting, ottoman, table.
The bookshelf stored Billy Bunter, King Arthur,
Friday night, our special tribesmen's palaver.

Multiplication learned by repetition,
Winning prizes for speed in competition.
Slates were used for numbers and the alphabet,
With crayons we drew a horse-drawn wagonette.

At Sunday School they tested our Bible gen.
Girls' choice text 'I will make you fishers of men'
Matched by the boys' verse 'At night they caught nothing'
Best of all Whit anniversary singing.

Venturesome exploits by the River Derwent,
Spotting flashing kingfisher's blue-green brilliant,
Then knickerbocker-glory ice cream sundae,
Made a memorable, frolicsome Saturday.

Jolliest annual event was Christmas,
With presents, turkey, plum pudding so scrumptious.
Plus a home-cine show of Charlie Chaplin,
With a bowler hat, walking like a penguin.

James Leonard Clough

FRIEND TO A FAILURE
(dedicated to my daughter, Karen, and her husband, Stephen)

You were there all the time as large as life
I took you for granted though
Never thought for a moment you'd be the one
To raise me again from below

Failure had come no one wanted to know
Their closed doors to me would endorse
Death called and in my unbearable pain
Decided a cowardly recourse

Failing even in that and angry when I awoke
Bewildered and in a strange bed
You visited me and picked me up
Then off to your own home you led

You cared for me there and protected me
Gave me all that I ever requested
And asked for nothing in return
Save to accept love freely bequested

That act of kindness lifted me
And still to my affections plead
Whenever I find a broken soul
I must encourage them in life to succeed.

Jim Carson

Untitled

    Oh,

                                                   What a beautiful day,
                                                          Children,

Picnic and play,

                  Cartwheels in the grass,
                  Echoes,

                                                              The wind,
                                              Carries their laughs

                           Afternoons,

In the park,

                                                                 Flies by

A lark,

                                                    One last memory,
                                                        Of the past,

                       Summer again,

From one day to,

                        L a s t

James Henry Brown

SEEKING

My heart leaps, he approaches.
I rise to meet my husband, my lover -
Pain stabs, but now only for a moment;
We kiss, I sit, watch his face -
Nodding, smiling, laughing at all his jokes.
He asks me and I want to answer him;
I think, I seek, smile again.
Pictures dancing before my eyes, so real,
Yesterday, playing tennis, in the sun,
The grey skirt and red jacket.

I always liked that jacket.
Wakes week on the Isle of Man with my dad;
Faces, I know, faces, are out of reach.
A hand touches his, so lined,
The loose skin, the bones, the pallor, not mine?
I am with him again, walking, alive;
His spirits lift me like wine.
All too soon he rises to leave, my joy.
The pain returns as I cling on to him;
Can this old man be my son?

A J Butterworth

HE GAVE ME GRACE

He gave me grace, unending love,
unsurpassable,
gift from above,

With tears gone, at sorrow's end,
I lost my life,
I found a friend,

Old things have gone, the new has come,
my spirit soars,
the battles won,

A chance to live, a brand new start,
He gave me grace,
out of his heart,

Rebecca Coombs

DIVE IN DEEP

Strangely the sun still shone,
Yet the light had gone.
The silvery moon rose silently,
Over the ebbing sea.
Deep beneath the festering surf,
The home of Captain Nemo's birth,
A tentacled octopus lay sleeping,
Amidst his pearly lair.
One droopy eyelid flashed,
As overhead the thunder flashed.
Sea anemones, clung lifeless,
As the marauding jellyfish danced.
A wandering angler took a chance,
With his pointed lance,
Took the bait line and sinker,
The fish swim in so many ways,
Without uttering a word to say,
Clowns and neon's sparkling whirl,
Bulging eyes mirror a strange face,
The diver turns vanishing with out trace.
An invader in the ocean scene,
Where all lay sublime and serene.

Scott Turner

PREFERRED IMAGES

Footprints in the virgin snow on a busy street;
Shrubs and ancient annuals of subtle shadow;
Jewels underfoot which vanish at a touch,
The sombre, sullen presence of cathedral-
Visions of a childhood lost in time.

Slipping, sliding . . . scrunching eyes shut against freezing sleet;
Thrusting cold hands into pockets far too shallow;
Courting mother's *lee* - not benefiting much
Before being hauled back under watchful eye -
Visions of a childhood lost in time.

Roasting *praties* at a bonfire, basking in its heat;
Rat-tat-tatting strange front door - knockers on a dare;
The warming coated arm which I loved to clutch;
The cousins met when someone old would die -
Visions of a childhood lost in time.

Holding hands on outings - the sandwiches we would eat
When picnicking on summer walks as a lad . . . oh,
Sweet islands in a stormy sea - and, as such,
Are preferred images when I recall
Visions of a childhood lost in time.

Perry McDaid

SIX MONTHS CLEAN

Six months ago my life was in turmoil, all because I was in denial
I was physically, mentally and spiritually 'all at sea'
I'd been running all my life from wanting and getting to know me.
Things didn't start changing for me until,
I put down drugs and started to do God's will
He's a God of my own understanding, not one of punishment,
He's not too demanding
The life I've got back is really God's gift
In the last six months I've reaped the benefit;
By giving out love and receiving it back
This simple thing keeps me on the right track.
I now live my life just for today, and seek to enjoy it in every way,
Many people have trusted me in such a short time
While I always thought I wasn't worth a dime
They came to me and checked if I was able to cope
Encouraging me never to give up hope.
Using drugs, for me, now has no meaning
All they would do is suppress my true feelings.
My life has been one of 'wheel and deal', now I can look at things
                                                                                       for real
From a life of self-pity and one filled with hate
Now it's the simple things in life I fully appreciate
For the first time in my life I can smile and laugh
Because I now know I've chosen the right path
Six months ago I was emotionally torn
I feel the real me has now been born.

Twinny

LOVE ETERNAL LOVE

You're the light at the end of my tunnel,
The truth that sets me free.
You're my strength and hope in troubled times,
And the only one
Who truly understands me.

You never let me down,
Never fail me.
You're always there when I need you
And you're my truest, most loyal friend,
The one person I can never do without.

And when life gets too hard for me
And I feel like giving up,
Your soft and tender voice spurs me on
To rise above my greatest obstacles,
To turn my greatest defeats to victories.

I love you and always will,
My one true and noble friend.
I need you by my side forever,
My one true and noble friend,
For I love you and always will.

N Yogaratnam

THE GUARDIAN

They say everyone has a guardian angel,
To see them through their life,
To be their guide, help them decide,
And aid them in times of strife.

I had often pictured *my* angel,
He'd be very tall and wise,
With a halo of flowing golden hair,
And bright and loving eyes.

But, last week, I was out shopping,
And I tripped and had a fall.
I lay there, feeling *such* a fool,
I couldn't get up at all.

May passed by as I lay there,
But one man stopped to care,
Picked me up, put me in a taxi,
And gave the driver my fare.

I didn't get a chance to thank him,
But that night when I prayed,
I thanked God for sending *my* angel,
So swiftly to my aid.

And, when I get to heaven,
And all the names are called,
I'll know *my* angel instantly -
He's short . . . bespectacled . . . and bald . . .

G J Outhwaite

TO KEITH

With pen in hand and you in mind,
I seek in vain the words to find,
The perfect sonnet to impart,
Such depth of feeling in my heart.
I bare my soul so you can see,
How much your being touches me.
For you, my sweet and gentle man,
Inspire me like no other can,
My senses swim in sweet confusion,
As thoughts of you in wild profusion,
Cascade and tumble, crash and fall,
In a literary waterfall.
Inflamed by your exquisite love,
Which others long deprived me of,
This bird, once trapped, at last set free,
Reaches for eternity.

Elizabeth Mary McNally

FAITH HOPE CHARITY

Faith took a cruel blow, when uncertainty crept in;
   decency abandoned, and mauled by evil will.
Saw suffering in the maw,
   when hunger gnawed at the individual within,
   and craved to quench the raging fires of thirst;
Orphaned to a tempestuous strife,
   and disregard for human life.

Hope cast into the sea of despair,
   then saved from the craggy undertow
   and the surges of a ravenous torrent below;
For there stood the rock of salvation,
   the stormy darkness transformed to a pillar of light.
Then *faith* returned, and a clearer understanding of -
     The Way The Truth The Life

Charity smiled to see an enlightened horizon,
  a new feeling of gentle regard awakened -
  and her soulful face shone,
  touched by a new-born fervency.

       For now we all rejoice
       Through love and grace abiding
       And all with faithful voice
       Sing praises for God's favours;
       And through His saviour son
       Repentance bringeth pardon,
       Our yoke is lightened such
       That sin hath no dominion.

K C Thomas

OUR WORLD

When this world of ours did first see light.
There was only just Adam and Eve, his wife
'This indeed is paradise,' they said in delight
But up slid the serpent, so slimy and smooth,
Determined to create chaos where're it moved.

A red little apple so tasty and sweet
Did upturn its tranquillity to one of deceit,
The two first children, namely Abel and Cain
Did grow up so differently, one saintly - one vain.

Alas! the nation did multiply, and as it stood
There was far more evil than there was of good.
Life did not turn out as God said it should.
We would like to return to *Eden*. If only we could!

Sadie Williams

A Seed Remains

The margin of my childhood path
explodes in sun-fired gold

a gilt-edged invitation
is urging a response from me

for all the years that, Esau-like
I've garnered self-indulgently.

Around me autumn's alchemy
releases from my hold
the locust-waste and

taste of rising
risen smoke
touch of falling
fallen leaf
ignite my memory.

A world where we played
under doily-patterned shade
on tea-party grass, and

double-summer time
when long sultry hours merged
with dew dawning showers, and

hay-making days riding home
on a horse-drawn wagon
in a limb-glowing haze

I let the thoughts pass.

The stubble field of childhood loss
devours the dross

I see those ashes winnowed
far and wide; a seed remains

and I am satisfied.

Angela Butler

OLD MAN

The good old days.
He said were grand
Come Sunday afternoon
Off to the park and
Listen to the band.
Six shifts a week
he used to work
for nothing but a pittance
down dark wet coal mines
in disgusting conditions
a big pan of broth
made from scrag-end meat
this was his veritable feast
A couple of woodbines
and a pint of ale
Sheer luxury to him
after a hard day.
He never complained
just accepted his lot
his memories now
are all he's got

Meg Turnbull

IN THE MOUNTAIN OF MY DREAMS

In the mountain of my dreams,
Stands the Lord in higher realms.
In the valley of my sorrows,
Stands the Lord for new tomorrows.

God is just,
God is right,
Thinking always of my earthly plight.

Amen to Him,
Amen to all that.

Serving God is a joy,
And praising Him is a fact!

Paul Gainsford Bailey

LONELY

Lonely in the field,
Crying for help,
Lost and no faces to see.
Feeling very lost and all alone,
Never fear, God is near.
So do not fear, the Lord is here.

Victoria Wills (8)

REAL CHRISTMAS

Is Christmas just a time for you
Of presents, food and such?
Of worrying 'Is this enough?'
Or 'Have I done too much?
What can I give to so and so?
Oh help! I'd quite forgotten Joe.'
You wear a frown, and fret and fuss,
Whatever is there wrong with us?
Why, this is not what it's all about
Forgive us, Lord, we've left you out!
That holy baby, born to be
The Saviour, sent for you and me;
So just be still, while you recall,
The glorious, holiest, gift of all.

Nance Davies

HOPE
(after Drumcree III 1997)

Blindfolded,
Hands and feet
Shackled to a tree,
Guns poised towards her,
Hope stands helpless
Ready to die.

Before they shoot
She hears
A gentle flurry of wings
Of countless peace doves
Soaring around,
Others nesting above her
Rearing chicks
Of more and more doves -

The prayer of those hundreds
And thousands
Who won't let her
Die.

Kathleen Davey

Delta Moment: Egypt 1943

Hold this . . .

      the morning clarity of mind:
Bound joyfully to the delta greenery
And misty silhouettes of palms and oxen,
To the placid footsteps and the cries
Of children, ever wise and never lonely.

Willingly secured to the sweeping grace
Of Ibis birds . . . the spirit lifts,
According with the English songs
Of other birds in other days
The winsome mellowing of inherent exile.

Eric Smart

THANK YOU FOR BEING MY FRIEND

I remember those first few visits to you
not knowing exactly what to expect
but you gave me ample time and space
confident that I would pull through

you listened, and I had so much to say
slowly you overcame my initial resistance
men like me keep their feelings to themselves
besides, finger paints were for kids at play

praising my first efforts, as if I were a child
when I presented the finished work to you
making me talk about my tear stained pictures
provoking dark emotions until they ran wild

imagine my elation when I was allowed a brush
now I could paint the horrors trapped inside
gushing out through the portals of my mind
picking the right moment, without any rush

you encouraged me to write about my feelings
predicting that one part of me would ascend
while the other side gradually diminished
you stood firm, I was spinning and reeling

at last I was able to comprehend my grief
like looking through a mysterious window
you were there, helping me to chip away
at the person who lay dormant underneath

so now, the time has come for us to part
you will continue your good works I'm sure
helping those who find themselves in need
adieu and merci from the bottom of my heart
                thank you for being my friend

Michael D Kearney

A SILENT PRAYER

How often do we kneel and say,
'Thank you Lord for another day.
For the love that you give us,
and your blessing too.'
Where would we be, if
it weren't for you?
You guide us in our work and play.
Show us how to live life in the right way.
When we are worried or we are sick.
We pray that you will help us quick.
Never do we as we pray, say
'Hello Lord, how are you today
with all the burdens of the world on you?
Is there any way we can help you?'
Oh! No. Selfish mortals are we all.
Yet, we expect you to hear us
       when we call.

Doreen Petherick Cox

CHILDHOOD RELIVED

The fire's alight, curtains drawn,
Muffins for tea, these will spawn
Childhood memories.

A candle flickers, shadows on a wall,
A tread on the stairs, dragon's tall,
Childhood fears.

A thick yellow carpet, cowslips yield,
Daisy chains, picnics, summer's field,
Childhood joys.

Tents under blankets, pavement cracks
Not to be walked on, tig-tag and back,
Childhood games.

A ship in a tree top, a look-out post,
River, sea below us, bank the coast.
Childhood adventures

Older sister's dress, satin and smooth,
Colour for her cheeks, eyebrows removed,
Childhood envy.

Whispers on the landing, open bedroom door,
Santa is not wearing his red suit any more,
Childhood realisation.

'Anne of Green Gables', please spell it with an *e,*
Boarding schools, midnight feasts, all of that me,
Childhood dreams.

Tomorrow, a long way off, next year never,
Twenty was rather old, forty was - forever
Childhood suspension.

Life like a patchwork, shaped with memory,
Brought about vividly with muffins for tea,
Childhood re-lived.

Jean Bishop

JESUS

Just who is the man we all talk to
Everyone knows him, he's the one who sees us through
Some people don't bother to give him praise
Until they need help in these terrible days
So think now and then who helps you in sorrow
Just count your blessings and live for tomorrow
Easy to say is 'I do not need him'
Satan won't get me, I'm too fast for him
Until the day you are off your guard
Suddenly it dawns on you terribly hard
Jesus it is that helps all asunder
Everything he does makes us sit back and wonder
Satan is all over the world, you can see
Under the stones to the top of the tree
So gird up your strength for the one we all love
Just remember he is our Lord and Master from up above
Ease out the devil and let the Lord come in
Shut all the doors and let the Lord reign within
Until you are strong for the Lord a hundred percent
Seek out the Lord's house 'He does not charge rent.'

Bob Shepherd

STREET SONG
(A Christmas Carol)

'Away in a manger,
No crib for a bed'
I haven't a pillow
To rest my poor head;
Nobody cares if I
Lie here and die,
The world is my home,
And my roof is the sky;
The elements toss me
From pillar to post,
But uncaring people,
They hurt me the most;
Because I am shabby,
My clothes are unkempt,
They treat me with scorn,
With their looks of contempt;
They know not the reasons,
They know not my sorrow,
I've suffered today,
And I'm dreading tomorrow;
As they rush on their way,
And turn a blind eye,
Nobody cares if I
Live or I die;
'Away in a manger,
No crib for a bed'
I hope by tomorrow,
That I will be dead.

Dorothy Neil

A FINE WEEK

Oh lord hear my words I speak
For a Monday starts the week of work
A day I dread, but glad of its close,
For Monday always seems to be a long day

Tuesday does hold its moments
But much brighter than yesterday,
More of it too, so to speak
But still holding its same hours of the day

Wednesday does tend to get harder
Mid week blues do tell a tale
Each yawn, and closing eye we show
But try to hide from the view of others

Thursday's a winding down process that begins,
Gently letting us know that the week is nearly finished
Reminding us of the rest to follow, we hope to have
Which always seems to be miles away

Friday's a day we look to with gratification
On what has been achieved throughout the latter
The long queues we muster to, in hope our packets are large
For the work just carried out, so demanding

Saturday, a day maybe for overtime
But that's getting scarce these days
With so many others wanting it
And that's only just to survive in this day and age

Sunday, I leave to share a thought or two
For you, dear Lord, in the form of a prayer
To thank you for the week just gone by
With a view to also seeing tomorrow, for one day I won't.

S J Davidson

NO ORDINARY TREE

Its roots penetrate the earth.
They cannot be torn out by human effort,
Nor by ferocious, clanging beasts:
For this tree is mighty, ringed by years,
Nurtured, tended, loved, with a stature
Made to truly stand time's greatest test:
To take its place above the rest.

Indeed, a tree of life, not death;
A tree of strength, with branches widely spread,
Sheltering the weary and heavy-laden,
Until, refreshed, renewed, they take an onward step.
Encouraged by a rushing wind
The travellers journey on in power,
With lightened loads, they travel faster,
Needs now met by a loving Master.

For this tree, this plain, this ordinary tree,
This tree once stood upon a hill,
Its outstretched branch took weight, such weight
A burden almost, almost too great;
Yet it stood firm, and proud, and tall,
Impervious to the taunts and jeers;
Within its strength.
For at its centre, rude and bare
Witness, the bloom, pure, radiant, fair.

'It is finished' came the cry.
The tree groaned with completed task.
Now, only now, could rough wood weep;
Full-blooded, red, the tears that fell.
Ordinary? Not this crossed, plain trunk,
For the bloom held there, it neither fades, nor dies.
Gaze, gaze in wonder, love and praise,
God's miracle, with us, for the rest of our days.

Elizabeth McWilliam

PRAYER SHARE

I've come to share a prayer, Lord,
as day turns into night;
Words are hard,
The thoughts are here,
Please help me get it right . . .

My friend at work has had an op,
Mum has had one too,
Bless them both
And let them share
The strength that comes from You.

My other thoughts unspoken, Lord,
You are already aware -
Your love encompass
All in need
Of the healing power of prayer.

As I now take my night-time rest,
O Lord, your blessing give -
Your light to shine
Your peace to know -
Another day to give.

Ann Voaden

THE PEOPLE'S PRINCESS - (1961-1997)

The nation's thoughts go out to you
To pass away suddenly seems so cruel
Work and love so freely given
Will carry on day after day
Smile of warmth Gave such hope
A spirit with loving light
Shall shine forever bright.

A Jones

THE DYING THIEF

He'd murdered and robbed for most of his life,
    Now he hung on a cross of shame;
He had been found guilty, the judgement was right,
    He had no excuse to complain.

But what of this man who hung at his side,
    They had called him *The King of the Jews,*
'Jesus,' he had heard of that name before,
    And of blasphemy this man was accused.

This Jesus spoke as they drove in the nails
    And said simply, 'Forgive them, Lord.'
How could he be so forgiving and kind
    While upon him abuse was poured?

The dying thief then began to think much
    Of his criminal life on this earth.
But this Jesus had helped others all of his life,
    He'd heard say he was good from his birth.

Another thief crucified on a cross
    Started to shout, mock and swear,
'Stop it!' the dying thief called out aloud,
    'This man's done no wrong, don't you care?'

The dying thief felt compassion for Christ
    He never thought could be true,
'Remember me' he said, 'when you come to your own,
    I would like to be there with you.'

Then Jesus spoke in words with such power,
    The thief saw that a new life could be,
'I tell you the truth,' the King of all kings said,
    'Today you'll be in paradise with me.'

Stan Mundy

NEEDLEWORK

Needlework is splendid to do.
It's beautiful to put on view.
Tapestry is row after row,
Embroidery is nice also.

Cross stitch can be so full of fun,
Coloured patterns really can stun.
It has a style all of its own.
It's so easy once you've been shown.

Embroidery is more complex.
Small stitches that can get you vexed.
Keeping it all even and flat
Chain stitch, satin stitch and all that.

Tapestry needs a lot of skill,
With patience and a good strong will.
Working from the bottom to top,
Once you start, you just cannot stop.

Masterpieces, you can get framed.
Perhaps, someday, will bring you fame.
But it's a lot of time you need,
To sit and do this worthwhile deed.

It's nice to make some presents too,
All quite unique, just made for you.
Large or small, I will work awhile,
And hope to make some people smile.

D M L Ranson

ALCOHOL- THE HIDDEN BEAST

When a marriage fades, and starts to die,
You look for answers to the question, 'Why?'
Could you have done more to make it secure?
No, you've done your best. Of that I'm sure.

You start married life with the best of intentions,
But redundancy can increase the tensions.
The breadwinner's depressed as he can't earn his keep,
Bills are mounting up, and the mortgage is steep.

The pressure is building, driving him insane,
So he drinks more alcohol to ease the pain.
His life has hit its lowest ebb,
Caught like a fly in a spider's web.

Through drinking too much, he's a victim of alcohol abuse,
Humiliation on the dole, is now just an excuse.
So mad at the world, he wants to hit out,
But being so drunk, it's the wife that gets the clout.

He wakes in the morning, not realising what he's done,
'Til he finds a note from the wife, saying she's gone.
You've thumped her many times, but this will be the last,
Any love she had for you, is a thing of the past.

As he now reflects on his lonely, sad life,
Remembering how he's caused so much trouble and strife.
Trying to recapture those far-off days,
When he wasn't looking at the world through a misty haze.

The wife's started a new life in another town,
Collected a degree, in her cap and gown.
He wants her back, but he realises it's no use,
Twenty-odd years down the drain - because of alcohol abuse.

Elaine Carver

AMOS BARKER

The Reverend Amos Barker rose from his knees
his church the meadow, his altar the trees
choir the birds, congregation the cattle
the surroundings of nature, against evil to battle
body of Christ an apple, water his blood
sermon of thanks knee deep in the mud
tirelessly roaming, his blessings to share
tending and helping the needy with care
his blanket the stars, his mattress the dirt
smiling and ignoring the hunger and hurt
like a shepherd of old, living close to his flock
watchful and sure, steady as a rock
with his bible as a shield protects all he surveys
protects them from evil's ravaging ways
at the end of the day, to the setting of the sun
this missionary gives thanks to the father and son.

A C Stock

THE GHOSTS OF OLD POEMS

I saw the ghosts of old poems
in quiet summer places,
I heard them rush past rivers
to be with old men fishing,
I saw them in the satin smiles of brides,
They stopped to be with angels
on green Easter mornings,
The ghosts of old poems lived
where winter left its loneliness in parks,
Bird by bird they came back in my heart,
but when I tried to write them down
I only wrote . . . God . . . beauty . . . love . . .

Marion Schoeberlein

I TO THE HILLS

When things go wrong in life and I'm perplexed
and wonder what will be, what's coming next?
My mind is filled with fear, my heart with sighs
    'I to the hills will lift mine eyes'

These hills were sheep and cattle safe do graze
unlike what man has made, are not a passing phase
Eternal - thy love has been, always will be
unlike the problems here below which trouble me.

Oh what a view I see from mountain tall!
Things large to me down there, now seem so small,
Life's difficulties, I now don't find confusing
the little things that bothered me, I now find quite amusing.

Safety I find up here from those who would pursue;
hid in the rocks and caves, well out of view;
refuge I find from those who would me hassle,
these hills become my fortress and my castle.

When I stoop down to drink from gentle brook,
I see reflected there your shepherd's crook
reminding me, where're I go,
still ponds, refreshing streams will flow.

Good though it is to sit and rest awhile
to scan the hills and seas for many a mile
I must return to face the challenges below
fresh insights to impart, thy love to show.

So when a hill or mount I climb
to say a prayer, my heart incline,
bring psalms of praise straight from the heart
to sing hymns like, 'How Great Thou Art.'

Ian Meredith

The Cross

Each step he took was a step of pain,
He was beaten, spat on, humiliated and shamed.
The cross that he carried was heavy and sharp,
Splinters of wood pierced into his arm.

Everyone shouting 'What's going on?'
Not everyone knew, this was Father God's son.
The road was long, the pain hard to bear,
But worse was to come, at the place prepared.

The nails were thick, each blow sent them through,
A crown of thorns on his head they put too.
Insects and flies swarmed at the smell of his blood,
To swot them away, if only he could.

He looked at his mother, remembering the times,
She held him close as a child when he cried.
Young lads were laughing - they thought it was fun,
If only they knew this was our father God's son.

Two criminals were placed, one on each side,
'We're guilty of crime and deserve death,' one cried.
'But you have done nothing, no guilt for this pain,
Forgive me, Lord,' one cried with shame.

Jesus gave his spirit . . . 'It's finished,' he cried . . .
Sixth hour, the sun disappeared from the sky.
The curtain in the temple was torn in two,
My Jesus has died for me and for you.

But that was only the start, you see,
He had gone through it all for you and me.
The love he gave was his life on that tree,
No favourites . . . no class . . . no culture . . . no creed.

The cross is the place new life must start. Jesus will give you a
>willing heart
It's no good pretending you can do it alone. Ask God today, come
>kneel at his throne.

These are the words God put in my heart, I was trying to really look at
>all my Lord went through on that day,
The heat of the day, the pain, the thirst, the shouting abuse, the sadness
>in his heart,

After all the miracles and love, we still could not believe.
Oh my Lord, please forgive us . . .

J Whitehouse

MEMORIES

Oh, happy childhood days
When I would wander
Thro' dew-drenched fields, and over yonder
To the wood with trees so tall
Whose branches like a blessing fall
Over leaf strewn earth, to cover all.

Where sunlight and shadows played
On fresh green bracken there
And honeysuckle with perfumed flowers
Rambled everywhere.
Where earth smells damp, bluebells grow
and violets so sweet
While dainty ferns and celandines
were crowded at my feet.

The trees with spiders' webs all hung
Each one with silver thread new spun
A butterfly would brush my cheek
As though some tryst with me would keep
A blackbird on some bough would sing
And babbling brook with laughter ring.

And all the love of things long past
Hurry thro' my mind so fast
As once again I see so clear
The precious things I hold so dear.

Maimie Stokoe

HEART REVIVAL

So much can happen that breaks our hearts -
Yet who's to know just how it all starts:
With confusion mixed through whims and trends;
Or inconsistent cultures and friends;
But if experience builds veneer,
It's to harden hearts, to conquer fear,
Then barriers of tension and pride
Crack into partnerships to divide -
And then who knows how to call a halt?
(Though what happens may not be our fault)
So how can we grow in truth and trust,
Without rules to govern greeds or lusts?
So much keeps happening in our time,
But hardened hearts cannot see - they're blind.

It's when the world makes us feel like dust,
That God can move to melt our crusts:
The dark, hard stuff encasing our hearts,
With all the grott that caused them to smart;
The stinging wounds that have made us run . . .
Though Christ conquered that, for everyone:
Regardless of the depth of our pit,
He championed Hell, to pull us from it!
And His pure heart, undamaged by pain,
Will resolve our whole, through grace not blame:
We leave the past with no value there,
As life with Him is beyond compare;
To overcome both our fears and woes,
Christ both fills our needs and takes the blows!

Natalie Brocklehurst

OUR LIFE ON EARTH

Our life on this earth has a purpose,
although the meaning is not always clear,
But we have our shining example
as the Christmas season draws near.
For that baby born in a stable,
was sent by Heaven above,
To teach us to live together,
in harmony, peace and love.
We were given those ten commandments
for us to read and obey,
but life is not always that easy,
and often we go astray.
But if we regret our wrong-doing,
and live our lives as we ought
From these good examples,
our children will be taught
Effort must be made by this human race,
to make our world a far happier place

Margaret Meadows

BEHOLD THE LAMB OF GOD

I gaze upon the dying form
of Christ the Lamb of God;
Then bow my head and humbly say -
How could you love me so?
Your bleeding hands and feet and side -
Such agony I see!
I don't deserve the price You paid
To set the sinner free!

I gaze into the empty tomb
Of Christ the Lamb of God;
Then lift my heart and praising say -
Your death has ransomed me!
You paid the price for all my sins,
Then rose triumphantly!
Although I don't deserve Your love
Praise God - You rose for me!

Vera Smith

In Your Hands

Oh God above please weep with joy
Do not this fertile land destroy
Fill the rivers, lakes and streams
Banish drought and drown her screams
Give the fish a place to dance
And take away destruction's lance
Be merciful and hear our call
Let raindrops soon upon us fall

Divinity whose love we know
Caused everything on earth to grow
Do not forsake us, bless our lives
With water show that your love thrives
Our life and death rests in your hands
Dry not rich soil to barren sands
Our throats are parched, our voices call
Let raindrops soak us as they fall

Lord above look down, please do
And help our priests, the chosen few
Who guard the waters that we buy
Of which reserves are running dry
Cleanse their hearts of greed, ensure
Their interests are for all quite pure
Let them do their duties well
That reservoirs once more might swell

Kim Montia

HIS EVERLASTING ARMS

The right arm of the Lord upholds me
When I am fragile and weak
The loving presence of my Father
Uplifts my soul
Enfolding my frail form
He lets me rest:
'Be still, my child'
The Sovereign Lord keeps me safe
He stays on guard for me
The Lord himself is my comfort
He restores power
Giving stability to my mind
He teaches me to climb with sure feet
While I lean into His everlasting arms.

Teresa Steele

WINGS OF AN ANGEL

Amidst the darkness, candles glowed bright
Sad were my thoughts whilst I strove through the night
Round, smiling faces of angels in flight
Uplifted my heart, no more would I fight

Discreetly I followed a path of delight
Through colourful paved gardens; of geese in flight
Shadows danced - night stars shone bright
Trees leant on a breeze, leaves reflected moonlight

Shimmered a meadow at dawn's first light
Golden buttercups, in their thousands stood sprite
The song of a blackbird, echoed delight
Wild berries of autumn, were plentiful and ripe

Amidst the darkness, candles glowed bright
The fairest of angels stepped forth from the light
Gleefully she smiled, my hand she grasped tight
Together we fled, toward Heaven in flight

Past a galaxy of stars and beyond, to pure light
Wings of an angel gathered speed in the night
Thoughts of ones past were dwindling - were slight
At journey's end - God's Heaven, we sight

Gerry Howsin

EASTER

What does Easter really mean
To a follower of Jesus
That man supreme?
It's not the chocolate
Or the rolling of eggs.
It's to remind us that Jesus died
And forgave us our sins.

The cross, the pain
That He had to bear.
He died in our place
And our sins he forgave.
The denial, the abuse
That He had to hear.
People turning their backs on Him
Wishing they weren't there.

Three days later
He was to rise again.
The empty tomb
And the stone rolled away.
People rejoicing
As He came their way

Heather Graham

On The Beach

On tasting salt sea spray
Warm air caressed my skin
Creation's healing hands
Held me, and drew me
Into the Creator's embrace

And the sand, soft and moist
Beneath my leaden shoe bound foot
Gave way its unsullied form
To receive my imprint
Like love's first kiss.

And some eyes may have seen me there
And considered me alone, forlorn
Not knowing that behind, beyond and between
The swirling mists of unsettled thoughts
Lies one undeniable;
God is love.

Paul Sherbird

GOD'S ANSWER

Each night I talk to our Father in Heaven, before I go to sleep.
I tell him of all my problems with tears. He answered and said
                                              'Do not weep'
'But, Father,' I said in deep earnest, 'Why is all this happening to me?
Why all the troubles and suffering? When will they let me be?'
'My child, dear child' God answered, 'Why do you so complain?
It's all a part of life, you see, your suffering and your pain.
So do not despair, 1 am with you. I'll be your light and your guide.
Be happy with each day I give you, for I love you. I'm right
                                              by your side.
So do not think of your troubles. My only son, he suffered too.
I do hope you haven't forgotten. He died on the cross for you.'
                                              Amen

O Savage

ONE YEAR OF PEACE IN NORTHERN IRELAND

The shimmering morning sun glowed brightly through the misty morn.
Heralding the dawn of day and drying dewdrops on the soft green
Grass with its warm refreshing ray.
Seeing that golden morning sun brought an inward peace to me
                                        and I thought
If Ulster's peace would last eternally.
Ulster no more the thorny path to tread or bombs or gunfire
Giving up their dead. No more we fear the noise of bomb or gun
Joy fills our hearts, we know that peace has won.
Then I thought of the judgement day
When at the portals of heaven, all will stand.
To be judged each one for their sin and wickedness,
and all the murders in our land.
Then the words of the Bible; came to me loud and clear.
Whosoever calls on my name, and confesses his sin
I will hear. Whosoever *will* can come to Jesus
And like the simplicity of a little child
Come in sorrow and repentance, meek and mild.
He will be forgiven. He will not be turned away.
God's holy word has spoken it and he will be forgiven
On that fateful judgement day. Then I saw the evening sunset
Spreading its gold and crimson wings across the western sky.
And the red sun slowly sinking behind the hills nearby
It is a year since peace was finally declared today
and in the stillness of the evening, in thankfulness
I humbly knelt to pray.

O Wylie

YOUR PRESENCE

Where are you when I need you the most.
On the steepest hills, you stood so close.
You never aided me, but stood along by
And for no action I wondered why.
But now I have learned the reason for
The way you made it plainly saw.
You're like a shadow that follows me,
You stand in silence, but you can see.
You are always there and taking care.
You give hope in total despair.
Your voice is silent, but your presence so loud.
Believing in you makes my being proud.
I cried out for you in the dark,
Your presence touched me and left its mark
And when I descend another steep hill
You're in my heart to give me will.
The will to climb; the will to reach;
The will to have a life of peace
And as a shadow you always follow
When my rivers are running shallow.
You carry on speaking your silent word.
You're in my heart, for at last I've heard.

Penelope Jayne Hopkins

A Thanksgiving For Light

There's so much light in this fair world
From stars and moon and sun,
We thank You, Lord, for all of it,
And also for the fun
Of fairy lights and fireworks,
Sunbeam on silver wave;
A rainbow in a waterfall,
And how glow worms behave.

But all this light by which we see
Is half the time not there,
For when night comes, it brings the dark,
When many say a prayer;
For the Bible says that dark and light
To You are both the same,
And that You'll always keep quite safe
Those who call upon Your name.

And so we thank You most of all
For Christ, the World's true Light.
Who came to bring the gift of faith,
That makes our lives more bright.
For once we have His light within,
Then we must surely know,
Whatever troubles come to us,
Safe through the world we go.

Elizabeth Mary Crabtree

A Prayer - With All My Love - Meg

Little hands clasped together, laughing eyes shut tight,
On bended knees by his bed, makes a touching sight.
Tries so hard to recall, his prayers to God above,
Asks Him for His blessing, and ends 'with all my love.'
'Now gentle Jesus can you see, the scar on my knee?
That's what I've got to show, for falling from a tree.
And did you hear me cry, 'cause I stood on my new toy?
Did you do naughty things, when you were a little boy?
If I'll be extra good, and mummy does agree,
If Heaven's not too far away - would you play with me?
I'll share all my toys - if you say 'Yes alright.'
And should it get too late, you can stay and sleep the night.'
Little hands holding tight, his ragged teddy bear,
Sleeping soundly till the morn, in the good Lord's care,
As I look upon my son, I feel a special love,
I gently kiss his cheek and say 'Thank You Lord above.'

Meg Brighton

WATCH AND PRAY

At the light of each new day,
Help us Lord to watch and pray.
At noonday in the fields of hay,
Show us Lord to watch and pray.
When the sun shines bright and flowers look gay,
Teach us Lord to watch and pray.
When success and happiness come our way,
Remind us Lord to watch and pray.
When troubles come and skies are grey,
Grant us grace to watch and pray.
And as the sun sheds sinking rays,
Guide us Lord to watch and pray.
Then when we kneel at close of day,
Lead us Lord to watch and pray.

Louie Conn

CIRCLE LINE

The sticks are dancing round the moon,
Tell us what for, I pray be soon.
Compassion, extinction, come what may
In the soggy winter we bathe Thy ray.

A ray of hope in minds forlorn,
A sweaty road, a bra-green lawn.
Try and turn, controlling force
Of the whirlpool, where its source?

On the cold grey pavement, by the grid,
Holy life-blood ebbs past Sid.
Destination? - in a twirl,
Gathering sticks just like a girl.

Save it! Save it, says a noise
The sticks are floating - they are boys!
Swinish hunger; stiff old chokers;
Sprawling cities, all at brokers.

Two sticks crossed in Crucifixion
For a man with Godly diction.
'Do Not Spit' - we see the sign
Of dirty fingers in the grime.

James Ivor Jones

A Cry From My Heart

A Cry to God

Why is it always the children who suffer?
Why do these little ones seem not to matter?
The kids of Blon are of such tender age,
Doesn't it fill You with anger and rage
That these children are seemingly just cast aside
On the whim of a government trying to hide?

Why, O God have You let all this happen?
Why is the graveyard full of these children?
You told us You were a God of love,
But how can You look on these kids from above
And see their hurt and the pain in their eyes
And do nothing, just sit there as cold as ice.

Why don't You do something? Why don't You care?
Why is the life for these kids so unfair?
They don't deserve it - what have they done
To bring all this suffering down upon them?

Please can You answer - if only in part,
Please respond to this cry from my heart.

God's Response

If you could see the tears in My eyes
When I see the pain in these little ones' lives.
If you could see just how much it hurts
To see My creation being dragged through the dirt.
If My mind could be opened, and My heart laid bare,
You'd know for yourself just how much I care.

The pain in this world was not by design,
I made this world perfect, it would have been fine
If man had not sinned, and carried on sinning,
'Tis man that has brought about all this suff'ring.

The communist state said, 'There is no God'
So don't be surprised if they ride rough-shod
  Over all My compassion, all of My care
And bring about almost unending despair.

But enough of the past - what about now?
I say I am helping - you still ask Me how?
  O why can't you see what it is that I do?
I choose to work through people like you.

That's why people travel for 2,000 miles
That's why the staff have always a smile,
  That's why the little that you can do
Can make such a difference - 'cause I'm in it with you.

Mark Barnes

FIELD OF DREAMS
(Isaiah 35 v 1-3)

I found myself within a field, but not of corn or wheat
Crocus blooms surrounded me, a carpet for my feet
and at the far end of the field, a sight that made me sigh
for there were many sunflowers standing six foot high.

A field of dreams it seemed to be, I didn't understand
and then a man beside me, took me gently by the hand
'Walk with me a while' He said 'and I will tell you why
you're in this field of crocuses and sunflowers six foot high

The crocuses are blooming now and each one holds inside
Saffron, my most precious spice, valued far and wide
You are like the crocus, holding something deep within
equally as precious - My grace - to help you win

For as you crush beneath your feet, the crocus sweet and fair
You'll see the blossom die - but the saffron is still there
and as you walk in life's rich field and suffer many trials
My grace will ever strengthen you and change your tears to smiles

And when you've walked across that field, and seen your life unfold
You'll rest beneath the shade, of the sunflowers' vibrant gold
And then within your field of dreams, you will clearly see
My precious gift of grace within, has brought you victory.

Carol Carthy

BORN ABROAD

Home is where the heart is.
A cliché perhaps; nonetheless the truth.
These words wistful cut if you've been severed
From your roots.

Home is more than buildings, we all know that.
The house is not the home. It's more than walls that
Hold us till we venture on our own.

Home is not a group of people known to us
As kin. With bonds of blood for mortar their births,
Deaths form the bridge spanning our life's waters.

Home is not built on memories - treasures in our
Mind or heirlooms kept since time. Neither eyes nor
Hands can hold dear what's most valued in our life.

Home is not localed in history where ancestors great
Were honoured with plaques on walls. It's not these
Monuments ascribing worth that keep us standing tall.

Home is not a place built or bought, lost to war or
Handed down. It exists where past and future meet.
Home is an appellation timely inscribed
When our heart's at peace.

Christine-Louise Secretan

THE TREE

Of all the things my Father made,
My favourite is the tree.
So tall, so strong, so elegant,
Its beauty all can see.

They stand, majestic, on the hills,
Down in the valleys too.
All different shapes and sizes,
Greens, golds and russet hue.

They stand alone in gardens,
Down street and avenues,
Or thickly on the hillsides,
Covering every view.

Their trunks are strong and sturdy,
They stand through wind and storm,
Shedding their leaves in autumn,
Leaving their naked form.

But when the spring comes round,
And the delicate twigs bear leaves,
What a wonderful web of colours,
The sunlight, dancing weaves.

Much like our God, Himself,
Tall, strong and everywhere.
Powerful and indestructible,
With arms our burdens to bear.

Alma Taylor

MOSI-OA-TUNYA
(Smoke that thunders)

Entranced I stood
 Silently gazing
  At the surging power of the water cascades.
  Rushing, rushing
   On and on,
     White water gushes uninterrupted from its course.
      Breathtaking force pulsates;
       Thunderous applause.
        Resounding sound carried by the wind.
         Regal columns of foam
          Boast incredible scenes.
           Endless floods pelting over a rollercoaster of rocks;
           Throbbing, pounding
            Without mercy.
             Roaring smoke - a furnace of water.
            Billowing clouds of spray,
            Climbing high,
            Reaching for the limitless sky.
           Aqua drops tossed vigorously
          From the brewing whirlpools below.
         A damp, humid smell fills the air;
        Heavy, yet refreshing.
       Majestic cataracts steaming,
        'The Victoria Falls' - incredible pillars of beauty.
       An awesome sight . . .
      A probing question:
      No God?
       Proof surrounds us;
        Creation's testimony.
       Lift up your eyes! And see.

Zoé Hodges

GENTLE MARY
(An Introit For Mothering Sunday)

Gentle Mary, she elect of
  Heaven, Jesus Christ to bear;
For her throne a lowly stable,
  Yet Queen of Mothers everywhere.

The favour of the Lord is with you,
  Gabriel's message was to her;
Happy she in contemplation,
  Later came the gift of myrrh

Honour Mary, gentle mother,
  Though joy and sorrow both her share.
Voices raise in salutation
  To honour Mothers everywhere.

John G Kingsley

FROM MY SITTING ROOM WINDOW

I sit here lonely, then I see
That God's hand is working, showing me
Of His wonders, of the setting sun
A scene that should move anyone
The barren trees show off the sky
That now is red, while clouds roll by
I cannot share this lovely view
But wait Lord, yes, I can with you.

For many years I've seen this view
Yet, always I find something new
Trees, be they green, gold or bare
Is God's own work, spread here and there
The clouds in their grand formation
Showing me Our Lord's creation.

Rena Slack

A Post Christian-Era Lament
(Why is it so difficult, so painful for our hearts to love Him? . . . Racine)

Why Son of Mary can't we be
Like brave St Peter was to thee
Knowing a love as strong as he
Who died on an upturned cross
for thee

Or why can't the light that blinded
Paul
A Pharisee they once called Saul
Hasten to heal sectarian hate
On brazen street of modern state

Or reach the harlot made to cower
Before a dealer's fatal power
And bid her leave his murderous
coil
To anoint thy feet with spikenard oil?

Is it because the mire's too deep
The saving path too hard and steep
That Christian Bunyan's hero trod
To reach the city fair of God

Or has the Church itself defamed
The glorious vision once proclaimed
Selling its sweet and sacred Trust
To Borgia's pride and Henry's lust

Or is soft comfort the winding sheet
That cramps the heart and binds the
feet
And makes us fail to hear thy call
Beyond the safe suburban wall?

Whate'er the shape of modern foe
Apathy, vice or libido
'Tis sad that saint and martyred maid
For our disdain so dearly paid.

Sarah Knox

Faith

Let not your heart be in despair
Days of sadness do not compare
Be like a child, trust and wait
For things written on Life's slate.

He promised He would never go
Too far away, of this we know
Weak or strong, this He does see
Looking into our heart He knows us to be.

Watches effort; seeing us win
Faith for keeping this for Him.
He recognises each of our ways
Carrying them with us every day.

With faith we do mentally grow
Learn things of which to know
Achieves much along with hope
Life is a road with many a slope.

Hannah Birch

ONLY A PIECE OF CLAY

Only a piece of clay
Cast on the potter's wheel.
Marred by a worthless potter
As he carelessly watched it reel.

Twisted and bent and broken
Only a worthless heap.
When along came the master potter
And a silent tear he did weep.

As he looked at the twisted vessel
That should have been something grand.
Gently he stopped the wheel turning
And he gathered it up in his hand.

Only a piece of clay
Cast on the wheel once more.
Gently twisted and moulded
Not like the vessel before.

Lord I am twisted and broken
Cast me again on the wheel
Gently make me and mould me
Put on this vessel your seal.

Then when the turning is over
And the wheel is silent and still.
May I be your beautiful goblet
Or just a mug, as you will.

Henry Armstrong

GOD AIN'T DEAD

A careworn woman
In cream anorak and peroxide hair
With cigarette which glows in the rain
Walks past me.
She's been told that
'God is dead'
And lives her life to that ideal,
And tells her kid the same.

She believes the angels left,
To ride the plastic flume,
She believes she's been abandoned,
And Nietzsche sealed her doom.

But if she'd sit with me awhile
And read my little verse
Maybe she'd find that
'God ain't dead'
In spite of Nietzsche's curse.

Why believe that God is dead,
Unless mankind is too?
And why believe that man is dead
Unless it's really true?
And if you find that man is dead
How can you think at all?
But if you find a mind one day,
Then tell me - woman sullen
Is God really dead?
Or are you missing something?

Colin E Amey

THOUGHTS OF FREEDOM

Through the bars I glimpsed the sky
The distant scene looked dazzling bright.
My captors were of myself -
Feeble flesh and tormented mind.
I needed strength to help myself
To release the bolts that held me in.
Relief appeared to come
A powerful blend of love and strength
Pushed the door open wide.
Hope streamed in as my hand reached out
To clasp the one
Who beckoned me to take the step
To leave the cage and
Not look back.
But the enemy heard the sounds of
Expectant faith and joyous hope and
Hastened up and slammed the door
Laughing loud with taunts and jeers.
Now the clouds descend
The prison walls close in and
Thoughts of freedom
Remain a dream.

Julie Howick

PREACHING TO MYSELF

I preached of stumbling blocks,
Of loving others, of building one another up.
But what of my own actions Lord?
I hurt those closest to me . . .
The things I should, I do not;
The things I should not, that I do.

I was tired, I was justified, I was in the right.
No - I was the one who spoke.
Me - I was the stumbling block.
And now I feel so guilty . . .
The things I should I do not;
The things I should not, that I do.

You were teaching me today Lord.
As I spoke from that high pulpit
I was preaching to myself.
It's me, it's me, it's me O Lord,
Standing in the need of prayer.

I asked forgiveness - made my peace,
Tried to build where I destroyed.
But there's a weight - sits painful on my chest.
Forgive me Lord for I have failed again . . .
The things I should, help me to do;
The things I should not, help me to resist.

Help me to know that I'm forgiven,
Help me to forgive myself, to start again.
I long to love as you love,
Always to practise what I preach . . .
The things I should, help me to do.
The things I should not, help me to restrict.

Val Flint-Johnson

SILENT WINGS

Dear Lord, we bow our heads before You.
Through us allow Your light to glow.
Be merciful to us Your children,
Please let Your loving kindness flow
On ever silent wings.

When trials and troubles flood our lives,
Compassion far beyond our gain,
Self-confidence seems so elusive,
Your love will flow to ease the pain
On ever silent wings.

When sin overshadows all the goodness,
Transgressions fill our hearts with woe,
In trepidation we will pray that
Your grace to us will always flow
On ever silent wings.

Then in our final hour on earth,
Each candle flickers once and dies.
When death's dark mantle covers over us,
Our souls at last to heaven will rise
On ever silent wings.

Morag Oag

PREPARE FOR WAR
*('Finally, be strong in the Lord and in His mighty power.
Put on the full armour of God so that you can take your
stand against the devil's schemes.' Ephesians 6 : 10, 11 (NIV))*

Put on your armour,
Prepare for war.
There is a fight now
More than ever before.

With breastplate of righteousness,
Faith as a shield,
The Word as a sword
So no ground we yield;

Helmet of salvation,
Readiness to preach,
The belt of truth
And the world to reach.

Our weapons aren't carnal,
They're mighty through God;
And they will pull down
Every stronghold.

We need to be militant,
To make a stand;
And forcefully advance
God's Word in our land.

Caroline Mortimer

PATTERN OF LIFE

The mist hung limp and soggy
Its tendrils moving slowly through bare branches,
Dragging wet fingers across the autumn grass,
Silently searching the mass of space.
There was no race - until the sun's rays began to steal,
In pale gold beam, its gentle way.
Lightening the shroud of grey
Persuading it to flee.
So each clammy finger melted in the light
Leaving in its wake drops of crystal
Clinging to the spiders' webs,
Showing patterns so perfect and yet so different.
And so with each life spent in God's shaft of love
The fears are banished and jewels shine,
His light perfecting His own design
In a life set free.

Betty Furneaux

A Blessing On The House

In this temple of peace and love
With earth below and stars above
The mind shall range its firmament
And love shall be its sacrament

Let none come near to cause offence
Or spoil the soul's munificence
Let all draw close who seek to bless
And know the touch of love's caress.

When all the blessed to earth can bend
Of suffering there will be an end
The heavens shall sound, and human ears
Vibrate to music of the spheres.

Then joy shall play its cleansing part
And peace shall enter every heart
The quest for truth will crown each day
And love alone shall guide our way.

Lesley Player

JUDAS

There is a path alone the pure may tread
I cannot take, although I take the Bread.
There is a path for those grace doth refine
I cannot take, although I drink the Wine.

There is a supper those with You attend
A meal to which the seeker may ascend,
And garbed and washed there, too, may be replete,
And still go to betray, with cleanséd feet.

There is a path for those who would betray
That's known to Him who is the Light of Day,
With others joined in worship with the Light,
    Yet eat the bread and go . . .
                      And it is night!

Deryck Mason

EVE OF CONSTRUCTION?

Our future is predicted
a code has been revealed
Will the sceptics be convicted
or truth again concealed?

        Encoded prophet's meaning
        for God has since replied
        a harsh computer screening
        that cannot be denied

A wordsearch may be faulted
but the writing's on the wall
The cynic's jeer is halted
before his rise and fall.

        The Earth's received its warning
        A Nation is addressed
        In signs of madness mourning
        It cannot be suppressed

The key is true repentance
for in the final hour
God will not pass sentence
but He will show His power . . .

        To an evil generation
        only Jonah is the sign
        Nations war with Nations
        before the end of Time

A new eve of destruction
this third millennium brings
A new chance of construction
'ere the ending of all things!

Down through time and history
Predictions have come true
This only leaves a mystery
The next one could be *you!*

Judy Studd

INFORMATION

We hope you have enjoyed reading this book - and that you will continue to enjoy it in the coming years.

If you like reading and writing poetry drop us a line, or give us a call, and we'll send you a free information pack.

Write to :-
 **Triumph House Information
 1-2 Wainman Road**

 **Peterborough
 PE2 7BU
 (01733) 230749**